E lizabeth I

Julia Holt

Published in association with The Basic Skills Agency

Hodder & Stoughton

A MEMBER OF THE HODDER HEADLINE GROUP

Acknowledgements

Cover: Portrait of Elizabeth I by Nicholas Hilliard (Photo AKG).
Illustrations: Mike Bell.

Orders: please contact Bookpoint Ltd, 39 Milton Park, Abingdon, Oxon OX14 4TD. Telephone: (44) 01235 400414, Fax: (44) 01235 400454. Lines are open from 9.00–6.00, Monday to Saturday, with a 24 hour message answering service. Email address: orders@bookpoint.co.uk

British Library Cataloguing in Publication Data
A catalogue record for this title is available from The British Library

ISBN 0 340 74727 7

First published 1999
Impression number   10 9 8 7 6 5 4 3 2 1
Year   2004 2003 2002 2001 2000 1999

Typeset by Fakenham Photosetting Ltd, Fakenham, Norfolk.
Printed in Great Britain for Hodder & Stoughton Educational, a division of Hodder Headline Plc, 338 Euston Road, London NW1 3BH by Redwood Books, Trowbridge, Wiltshire.

Contents

The year was 1603.
The month was March.
A 69 year old woman
was lying on the floor.
She didn't want to get into bed
because that would be giving in to death.
Elizabeth I was dying.

She was unhappy, bald,
with bad skin and black teeth.
But she was still the Queen.
The last of the Tudors.
Everyone must kneel to speak to her
even if she was lying on the floor.

Elizabeth had been
the Queen of England and Ireland
for the last 44 years.

As she lay dying
Elizabeth looked back over her life,
the good times and the bad.

In the last 69 years
her country had seen many changes.

It was a boom time in England
for art, music, poetry, trade, building
and most important, the theatre.
William Shakespeare was born
when Elizabeth was 31 years old.

It was a golden age
for England,
so good that it was named after her:
the Elizabethan Age.

1 Childhood

The old Queen looked back
to her childhood.
She was born in a time of trouble
for England.
The trouble was the struggle for power
between Catholics and Protestants.

Henry VIII changed the religion of England
from Catholic to Protestant.
He did this so that he could marry
his second wife, Anne Boleyn.
He wanted her to give him a son.
He needed a son to be king after him.

Elizabeth was born on 7 September 1533.
She was his second baby girl.
He was so angry
that he didn't go to her christening.

She was sent away from London
to grow up in the country.
This was normal for royal children
to keep them away
from the plague and the smoke.

As the little girl grew up,
she always boasted
that she was 'mere English'.
Both her parents were English
and she never set foot out of the country.
Her older half-sister, Mary,
was half Spanish and a Catholic.

Little Elizabeth was taken to London
to visit Henry many times.
He was her idol.
She looked up to him
all her life.

But when she was three years old
her life changed.
Henry had Anne Boleyn beheaded.
She had not given him a baby boy.

Henry said Elizabeth was illegitimate.
He sent her back to the country
with less money to live on.

Life was a bit better
when Henry's third wife
had a baby boy, Edward.
Edward came to live in the country
with Elizabeth and Mary.
Elizabeth loved her new half-brother.
She made little clothes for him.

All the royal children
were taught at home.
Elizabeth was taught
Greek and Latin at the age of 10.

For fun there was dancing,
riding, archery and sewing.
Mary taught Elizabeth to play cards.
They had a jester and an acrobat
to make them laugh.

As she grew up,
Elizabeth didn't see her father very much.
He was ill and full of self-pity,
but he was still her idol.
She was interested in his power
and what he did with it.

In a painting of the day
Elizabeth has a pale face,
a red dress and a few jewels.
But she does look very royal.
She has her books with her
to show that she is clever.

These were the calmest days
of her life.

King Henry VIII.

The calm days ended in 1547,
when Elizabeth was 14 years old.
King Henry VIII died.

He said that his children
should sit on the throne after him.
He named Edward first,
then Mary and then Elizabeth.

So Edward VI was crowned king.
But he was a sickly boy.
He died of TB at the age of 16.
He was only king for seven years.

Then it was Mary's chance to be queen.
She was crowned in 1553.

Mary tried to turn the country
back to the Catholic religion.
She married the Catholic King of Spain.
She locked Elizabeth
in the Tower of London
to keep her out of the way.
Elizabeth kept her life
by saying she was a Catholic.

Mary had so many Protestants killed
that the people called her
Bloody Mary.
When she died in 1558
the people were very happy.

Elizabeth was locked in the Tower.

2 Queen

It was now Elizabeth's turn
and she was ready.

At the time she was crowned
England was torn apart.
There were religious problems.
The country was poor
and it was in the middle of a war
with France.

Elizabeth was only 25 years old
and very vain.
But she knew how to rule.
She learned by watching others
over the years.
She knew she had to be careful
and choose the best advisors.

Elizabeth was quite tall for those days,
about 5 foot 4 inches.
She made her pale skin even paler
with a mixture of egg white and poppy seeds.
Her eyes were hazel
and her hair was red, until it fell out.
Then she wore a red wig.

Elizabeth was crowned
at Westminster Abbey.
As she walked on the blue carpet
the people cut off strips
to take home and keep.
They were so pleased to have her as queen.

In her first year as queen
the war with France was ended.
Elizabeth also made
the Church of England
the main church.

She made the people
proud to be English.
England became a great sea power
with heroes
like Sir Francis Drake
and Sir Walter Raleigh.

Trade with other countries
was promoted
and trade in England was supported.
Standard coins were minted
and prices started to fall.

Over all this was Elizabeth.
In the eyes of the people
Elizabeth *was* England.

One big problem
for Elizabeth and England
was that she wasn't married.

Her advisors were always
begging her to marry.
But she said,
'I will live and die a virgin'.
She became known as
the Virgin Queen.

This did not stop her
from offering to marry many men.
She always had her favourites.
But only when it gave her power.

Elizabeth cheated death
many times in her life.

When she was 29 years old
she had smallpox.
She was wrapped in a red cloth
for a week to stop the scars.

The doctor was afraid to treat her.
He had to be taken to her room
at knifepoint.

She was left with a scarred face.
So she hid the scars
with thick make-up
and didn't smile in case it cracked.

Elizabeth often had problems
with her teeth.
She only had cloths
and toothpicks to clean them.
But she liked very sweet food.

At 45 years old
she had toothache for three months.
But she wouldn't let
the doctor treat her.

The Bishop of London agreed
to let one of his few teeth be pulled
to show the doctor's skill.
Then Elizabeth let the doctor
do his work.

3 Plots

As long as Elizabeth lived
there were plots against her.

There were two Catholics
who said that they should
rule England.

The King of Spain
was Queen Mary's husband.
As soon as she died
he said he should be king.

Mary Queen of Scots
was Elizabeth's cousin.
She said that Elizabeth was illegitimate
and so she should be queen instead.

Mary Queen of Scots was executed.

When Mary Queen of Scots
came to England
Elizabeth had her locked up.
She kept her locked up for 19 years.
English Catholics tried to free her
many times.

In 1586 Elizabeth's spies
found out about a plot.
It was to kill Elizabeth
and put Mary on the throne.

Elizabeth was never very good
at making up her mind.
But she had to in this case.
Mary was executed the next year.

The King of Spain was so angry
that he sent his Armada to England
in 1588.
He hoped to join up
with the 25,000 English Catholics
and take over the country.
But his Armada was beaten
by the smaller English fleet.

Elizabeth went to the docks
to thank the fleet.
She rode a horse
and wore steel armour like a man.
She said, 'I may have the body
of a weak and feeble woman,
but I have the heart
and stomach of a king'.

Elizabeth had made England
and the Protestant Church
strong and proud.

She was a strong woman.
When she was angry
she did not mince her words.
She spat on the floor
and banged her fist on the table.
She was as powerful as her father.

So why was she dying alone and unhappy
15 years later?

4 The End of an Era

Elizabeth had outlived
her own golden age.
She had outlived her friends
and her best advisors.

The Irish Catholics
were in revolt against her.
England was still at war with Spain.

She had too much power
and her new advisors wanted some of it.
They were waiting for her to die.

She lay dying on the floor
until she was so weak
that she was put into bed.
Elizabeth I died in her sleep
on 24 March 1603.

Elizabeth never said
who should rule after her.
Who should sort out the mess
that she had left?

But even before the funeral,
James the son of Mary Queen of Scots
was making his way to London
to be the next King of England.

Elizabeth's body was taken
to Westminster Abbey.
The writing on her stone says,
'the mother of this her country'.
She was the first queen
to have an age named after her.